All material is for entertainment only.
Nothing is printed to offend. It is the belief of
the author that all people are to be respected
and no individual or group is inferior
in any way!

LIMERICKS, JOKES AND OTHER SUCH RUBBISH

by

Stanley J. St. Clair

ISBN 978-1-935786-73-3

Printed in the United States of America

St. Clair Publications
P. O. Box 726
Mc Minnville, TN 37111-0726
http://stclairpublications.com

Contents

Section One

Original Limericks

A young Irish lassie named Patty,
moved southward from old Cincinnati.
Because she was freckled,
she often got heckled;
but a red-headed Mickey went batty!

****

There once was a sailor called Sammy,
who was sweet on a wave name o'
Tammy.
Said he to she,
"Come flee with me!"
But she sent him home packin' to
Mammy.

****

A little ole lady o' Dublin,
sipped ale till her belly was bubblin'.
As she left from the pub,
her toe, she did stub,
'twas dreadful th' things she was
mumblin'.

A Scotsman abusing his scotch,
got so drunk he could nay read his
watch.
At two in th' morning,
with nary a warning,
he threw up all over his crotch!

****

A laddie, in lieu of 'is shamrock,
a lassie, did offer a ham hock,
"I'll think on it, miss,
if ye'll throw in a kiss,"
said the lad, so he gave up 'is shamrock.

****

A sneaky young lad called Marty
crashed rudely a beekeeper's party.
He was chased by the bees,
yelling, "Oh, save me please!"
Serves 'im right fur bein' a smarty!

Limericks, Jokes and Other Such Rubbish

Section Two

Jokes you haven't heard

TRUE STORIES OF THINGS KIDS SAID

I never liked Santa anyway

A three-year old boy was misbehaving about a month before Christmas. His mother spent several minutes explaining to him how important it was that he be good, because Santa was checking his list to make sure he should pay him a visit.

The boy frowned and looked into his mother's eyes. "I never did like Santa very much anyway."

****

Kindergarten retirement

A five-year-old boy came home from the first day in kindergarten, and his mother asked him how he liked school.

"I didn't like it," he grunted.

"Well, you'll get to know some other children and I'm sure you'll feel differently in a few days," she replied.

"Okay," he said, "I'll give it three days and if I still don't like it, I'm gonna retire."

****

Man down!

Six-year old: Mama, the TV said there was a policeman injured!

Mama: What happened, honey?

Six-year old: He was in that line where the bad guys shoot at them.

Mama: What line are you talking about?

Six-year old: I think it's called "the line of duty."

****

Upper case or lower case?

Mother to five-year-old: Look Johnny, there's a flock of geese flying overhead. They always fly in a V formation, you know.

Johnny: Upper case or lower case?

****

Spacebook

A four-year-old girl had spent the day with her grandmother while her mother and father were at work. When the father returned, the grandmother went home.

The mother called and asked the grandmother how it went. She told her that the little girl had been a perfect little angel that day. When the mother finally got home, she said to her daughter, "I heard you were a good girl for Nana today!"

The four-year-old cocked her head and replied smugly, "How did *you* know? Did you see it on Spacebook?"

****

OTHER ORIGINAL CUTIES

Proper Usage

A tenth grade health teacher was giving a class on use of common household medications. She asked the students to use the words allergy, X-lax, bathroom, headache, Benadryl, and Tylenol, combining them in such a way that she could know that they understood proper usage of each.

The class clown turned in the following illustration: *It's not that I have an allergy to her, but my X-lax personality. The last time I was at her house, I went in the bathroom, and she started yelling at me, and it gave me a headache. If my fist had Benadryl I would have torn the place apart, Tylenol.*

****

The Deaf Mutt

Question: How does a deaf dog sound when it barks?

Answer: "Moot! Moot!"

****

Dead Time

If you're in the market for dead time, I'm fairly certain you'll find it at Walmart. I've been in there killing it a number of times.

****

Adopted

Two simple country brothers were taken by a city cousin to spend some time with his family.

"Y'all got any kids?" one asked the city cousin.

"Just these two," he said, pointing to their dog and cat.

After leaving, one boy said to the other, "Ya know, their kids didn't look a thing alike."

"Naw," said the other, "One of 'em must be adopted."

****

Air Bag

A rookie cop was sent out his first day with a loquacious lady in blue. At the end of the day, the chief asked him to share his thoughts regarding his introduction to the job.
  "Everything was fine out there," he said, "but you didn't tell me that the driver-side airbag would be set off."

****

Plenty of Space

A growing restaurant had a sign directing customers to the additional parking behind the establishment. A prankster who was at odds with the owner decided to have a little fun. After hours he stopped by with paint and a brush and made an extra "S". The sign then read: "Sparking in the rear."

****

The Seamstress

Question:
What do you call a seamstress whose shop is in her basement?

Answer:
A low-down sew 'n' sew!

****

Skipping Curser

What's the difference between a cursing skipper and a skipping curser?

A cursing skipper picks a fight with a sailor.
A skipping curser makes a writer a failure.

When hell freezes over

An older Southern couple was cruising through Southeastern Michigan in January when they came upon a community sign which in large letters read 'Hell'. A sheet of icicles dangled from the bottom.

"Well," drawled the husband, "I'll be ordering my new Cadillac when we get home."

"What are you talking about?!" the wife protested sharply.

"When I told you I wanted one you said, 'Sure, when hell freezes over!'"

****

How ridiculous!

A man saw an ad where someone had a blue toddler seat and an underground dog fence for sale, and he thought. *How ridiculous! Who would want those things? I don't know anybody with a blue toddler or an underground dog!*

****

21

Redundancy

At six A.M. in the morning
As the sun arose, at the break of day,
I saw a Black Angus cow
Silhouetted dark against the rays;
Alone in a field, all by herself.
It was déjà vu all over again —
I'd been there before, but when had it
been?

****

Restaurant droids

This much is true: someone has invented a droid for delivering food to the tables in restaurants! My question is, "If my food is delivered by droid, do I tip the droid?"

****

Why do you ask that?

At the height of his scrutiny by the media, Dr. Kevorkian was interviewing a teen-aged girl to work in his office.

"What do you think of euthanasia?" he asked.

"Why do you ask that?" she returned, a puzzled gaze on her brow. "What's this job got to do with young people in China?"

****

If I had a million bucks

An elderly coal miner in West Virginia was driving his pre-teen grandson out to a fast-food joint in his pickup truck for his birthday. They pass by a classy restaurant and the boy turns to his grandpa and says, "Why don't you just take me *there*, being it's my birthday, an' all?"

The old man frowned and glanced back at the boy as he sped on by. "Why, that's not such a big deal, goin' there. If I had a million bucks for every time I'd e't at that place I wouldn't have ta worry 'bout anything fer the rest o' my life!"

The grandson raised his eyebrows. "Oh, really, Grandpa? How many times have you eaten there?"

The old man wrinkled his brow and stiffened his lips. Then he drawled in a low tone, "Onest."

****

Amnesia

An elderly couple had been in bed for half an hour and the husband was still tossing and turning.

"Why can't you settle down tonight?" the wife snapped.

"I think I've got amnesia," the husband groaned. "That's what you call it when you can't get sleepy, right?"

"Hmmm, I guess so," came the reply. "I can't remember."

****

Why don't people have tails?

Fish have tails to guide them in swimming.

Opossums' tails are wrapped around tree limbs so they can hang upside down.

Cows' tails are useful in swatting flies.

So why don't people have tails?

ANSWER:
People use their tongues to wag their tales.

Limericks, Jokes and Other Such Rubbish

Section Three

The Name Says it All

AUTOMOTIVE INDUSTRY:

Iona Carlotta Lemons – A buy-here pay-here auto dealer

Minnie Cooper –A gal who wants to show off her style in sporty little cars

Otto Parker – A professional parking lot attendant

BANKING:

Drew A. Pension — A retired banker

Rob Banks –A notorious hold-up man

ENTERTAINERS:

Bunny Hopper –An ex-stripper who opted for a more accepted profession as a dance instructor

Koh Ming Sun — A fabulous motion picture promoter whose name appears on many a marquis

Minnie Moore -A very versatile and popular performer who shows up for all major events, but inevitably receives bottom billing

Tony A. Ward — An actor bucking for attention

JEWELRY:

Jewel Hyder -A sneaky diamond store employee who steals the joint blind

Jim Stone — A prominent jeweler

Pearl Stringer — A jeweler who makes hand- crafted items

LESS DESIRABLES:

Allotta Manierre — A girl who always knows everything and isn't afraid to tell you

Ben Goode -A priest who took off his collar permanently

Buster Upchurch — An arrogant deacon who knows how 'God's house' should be run

Chris P. Cash — A counterfeiter who spreads his product around

Frank N. Stein — The creepy owner of a costume and party store

Harry Arms -A robust lifeguard with a bit too much body hair

Ima Hogg -The portly woman who pushes in front of everyone at the buffet

Jay Walker — A persistent ignorer of the crosswalk signs in midtown Atlanta

Jimmy Lockes — A petty thief on the bulletin board in the Post Office

Justin Case — A Hollywood attorney who specializes in pre-nups

Levy Malone — The second husband of a desperate ex

Lilly White – The daughter of a neo-Nazi

Mae Day — A girl who everybody warns the guys about

Rowe Ving Hand — A sneaky man looking for ways to lure women

Rusty Auld Irons – A stingy golfer who needs new clubs

Shirley A. Gooden — The third wife of a prominent politician

Terri Bull Cook — A young bride who never learned to boil water

Truly N. Justice — A scrupulous attorney defending the 'scum of the earth'

Ura Nutt -A cocky psychiatrist

MISCELLANEOUS:

A. Chance Love — A guy who bumped into a girl at the park and she asked him out that night

B. Goode Tumey — A guy a girl met on the rebound

Brad Seals — The fellow who shoots the rivets into the wings of airplanes

Carrie A. Lott — A hefty young lady working with Acme Moving Company

Dunn Eton — A weight loss expert

Hope U. Fine — A well-wishing letter writer

Ivy Clymer — A female window washer who can navigate the sides of tall buildings

John Works — A plumber who guarantees his jobs

Justus Goode — A representative who fights for underdog causes

Landon Safely — An award-winning pilot

Leo Lyons – An adamant astrologist born in August

Lucy Lastick – A tailor recommended by Jennie Craig to take up waist bands for women clients who have lost significant amounts of weight

Mark Downs – A sales clerk at Wal-Mart after Christmas

Peony Bush –A professional dog walker

Polly Shope-Silver — A restorer of old coins

Rosetta Stone — An interpreter of miscellaneous languages

Sonny Rey — An eternal optimist

Teddy Bayer — A cuddly man addicted to aspirin

Woody Barnes — A dealer in antique lumber

U.R. Best —Someone who wants to flatter you

PERSONAL HYGENE:

Curley Hare — A male cosmetologist

Harry Barber — A shop owner who doesn't take time to get a trim

OUTDOORS, HORTICULTURE AND RANCHING:

April Rose — A flower shop owner

Bambi Hunter — A cute young thing who goes after unsuspecting prey

Cherry Pickens — The curator of an orchard in Washington, DC

Chip Block — A woodcarver with great ambitions.

Dusty Trail -The owner of a dude ranch

Forrest Fines — A Park Ranger at Yellowstone

Georgia Clay — A Southern Bell into sticky propositions

Hill E. Land — A real estate developer in the foothills of Tennessee

Lon Greene — The owner of a garden shop in suburbia

Redd Mudd — A fellow who would like to get you bogged down in his ideas

Rosa Corn -The new proprietor of the 'Field of Dreams' farm

Rose N. Bloom — A nursery worker who prefers the flower garden to the home

Rocky Mount — A Colorado hiking guide

Sandy Beach — A gal who wants to have a good time and loves surfing

Spring Rains -A young lady who thinks the sun can't come up until she passes by

Stony Meadows — A failed cattle rancher in Montana

Summer Storms – A pal of Spring Rains who always seems to follow her, who is also known for chasing tornadoes.

Woody Cutter – A logger in the Pacific Northwest U.S.

PUBLICATIONS:

Arthur Bigg – A braggadocios novelist

Reed Moore – A book publicist

Rita Paper – Head of promotions for the *New York Times*

TRAVEL:

Ben Farr – A travel agent hawking his services on the beach

Burn Bridges – A man who moves a lot and never looks back

Hugh Argo Ing — An insistent ticket agent

I.C. Winters — An avid traveler who prefers to remain in International Falls in the colder months

SWEET THINGS:

Candy Apple — A carnival worker who runs a concession stand

Cookie Crum — A pastry lover who won't waste the tiniest morsel

Honey Combs –A bee keeper with a special talent for bee-ing sweet

Peaches Pitts — A young sweet girl on the surface who is really hard to the core

Rosy Cheeks — A model for a new cosmetic line

Section Four

Aye, ya gotta be a Scot Ta get it

From Iain Sinclair

Jokes that I think are only understood in Scotland (they have to be spoken to work):

Q. What does Bing Crosby do, but Walt Dis-ney?
A. Bing Crosby sings.

Q. Is that a pavlova or a meringue?
A. Na, you're right, it's a pavlova.

They will tune your ears to the accent.

****

From J.B. Sinclair:

SCOTTISH BLOOD:

An Arab Sheik was admitted to the best heart hospital in England for heart surgery, but prior to the surgery, the doctors needed a store of his blood in case of emergencies. As the gentleman had a rare type of blood, it couldn't be found locally, so, the call went out all over the country.

Finally a Scot was located who had a similar blood type. The Scot willingly donated his blood to the Arab.

After the surgery, the Arab sent the Scotsman as appreciation for giving his blood, a new BMW, a pot full of diamonds plus a cheque for £100,000.

A couple of days later, once again, the Arab had to go through corrective surgery. His doctor once again telephoned the Scotsman who was more than happy to donate his blood.

After the second surgery, the Arab sent the Scotsman a thank-you card & a jar of Cadburys fruit and nut.

The Scotsman was shocked that the Arab this time did not reciprocate his kind gesture as he had anticipated.

He phoned the Arab & asked him: "I thought you would be generous again, that you would give me another BMW, diamonds & money; but, you only gave me a thank you card & a jar of chocolate".

To this the Arab replied: "Aye, but I now have Scottish blood in me veins."

****

Bagpipes at Funerals, as related by a piper...

As a bagpiper, I play at many gigs. Recently I was asked by a funeral director to play at a graveside service for a homeless man. He had no family or friends, so the service was to be at a pauper's cemetery near Clifton south of Toowoomba. As I am not familiar with the backwoods, I got lost and, being a typical man, I didn't stop and ask for directions. I finally arrived an hour late and saw that the funeral guy had evidently gone and the hearse was nowhere in sight. There were only the diggers and crew left and they were eating lunch.

I felt bad and apologized to the men for being late. I went to the side of the grave and looked down and the vault lid was already in place. I didn't know what else to do, so I started to play. The workers put down their lunches and began to gather around. I played out my heart and soul for this man with no family and friends. I played like I've never played before for this homeless man.

And as I played 'Amazing Grace,' the workers began to weep. They wept, I wept, we all wept together. When I finished I packed up my bagpipes and started for my car. Though my head hung low, my heart was full. As I opened the door to my car, I heard one of the workers say, "I never seen nothin' like that before and I've been puttin' in septic tanks for twenty years."

Apparently I'm still lost.... it's a man thing.

****

Scottish wedding

A Scottish couple was getting married and invited all of their closest friends. As the priest was about to pronounce the happy duo 'Man and wife,' he said cheerily, "Now, I want all 'o ya ta get real close ta the one who holped ya's the most ta get through yer hard times!"

A muffled scream came from the back of the chapel as a great number of folks pressed hard up against one balding man.

"Who'r ye?" the priest sang out, unable to see him as he attempted to push from the press.

"I'm yer buddy, Can't ya see? It's Iain...the barkeep down at th' pub!"

Section Five

Dummies Disguised as Average People

True Stories of Thoughtless Humor

No Left Turn

I pulled up behind a lady who was stopped at a green light with her left blinker on, indicating that she was intending to enter the Walmart parking lot. There was no oncoming traffic to prevent her turn, but she sat out both the entire green light and the red light which followed. As soon as the left turn arrow lit up, she proceeded to turn. As she entered the lot, without slowing down, at two prominent NO LEFT TURN signs, she turned left again.

****

Accident Insurance

Some years back, a young lady contacted her insurance agent to file a claim for her pregnancy. When the agent checked her policy, he said with a frown, "You only have accident insurance, not maternity benefits."

"It was an accident," the girl answered, earnestly.

****

I'd like to Solve!

A lady on a national game show had an obvious puzzle all filled in but one letter. Excitedly she mis-solved.

****

Hydrant, please

Back in the flashy 1970s, a man wearing a bright red double-kit leisure suit was visiting in a home where the patrons owned a feisty male Chihuahua. After sniffing all around the visitor, the dog proudly hiked a rear leg and wet all over the red trousers.

"Get away from him!" the owner scolded. Then apologetically he said to his visitor, "Apparently he thought your leg was a fire hydrant."

47

****

Big Mac Attack

In a small town in West Virginia in the 1980s, a fire engine sped into the local McDonalds with the lights flashing, and sirens roaring, stopping at the drive-in window.

"Where is the fire?" the attendant asked excitedly.

"There's not one," came the nonchalant reply. "We were all having a Big Mac Attack."

****

Oh, deer me!

There is a story told of a lady in rural Kansas who called one of her neighbors about the uselessness of a road sign in the area.

"There are too many deer getting hit by cars out there," she said with genuine concern. "Someone should take down that DEER CROSSING sign. I don't think it's a good place for them to be crossing anymore!"

****

80% Chance of Rain

A young, uneducated boy was staring out the window of a church one drizzly Sunday morning, when another parishioner joined him.

"The weatherman said we had an 80% chance of rain today," the boy drawled. "I think he about hit it. It's raining about 80% of the time."

****

How much ya reckon that costs?

In a small town in the Southern US, a young cashier was beginning her first day at the grocery store checkout. The second customer had placed a divider between the items being purchased by the first customer and hers.

After finishing the initial customer's orders, the cashier picked up the divider and turned it all around in her hand, staring at it inquisitively.

"I wonder how much this is..." she said blankly.

****

I spotted a leopard!

Two men were on a safari to Africa when one remarked to the other, "Hey, John, I think I just spotted a leopard!"

"No, Sam," his friend snapped, "you didn't! They come that way."

****

SAME CATEGORY:

The following are forwarded emails which were meant to be shared. Well, I'm sharing, *but with all names of persons and specific cities altered!*

Yes, it's that magical time of year again when the Darwin Awards are bestowed, honoring the least evolved among us.

<u>**Here is the glorious winner**</u>:
1. When his .38 caliber revolver failed to fire at his intended victim during a holdup in Malibu Beach, California, would-be robber James Evans did something that can only inspire wonder. He peered down the barrel and tried the trigger again. This time it worked.

And now, the honorable mentions:

2. The chef at a hotel in Switzerland lost a finger in a meat cutting machine and after a little shopping around, submitted

a claim to his insurance company. The company, expecting negligence, sent out one of its men to have a look for himself. He tried the machine and he also lost a finger... The chef's claim was approved.

3. A man who shoveled snow for an hour to clear a space for his car during a blizzard in Detroit returned with his vehicle to find a woman had taken the space. Understandably, he shot her.

4. After stopping for drinks at an illegal bar, a Zimbabwean bus driver found that the 20 mental patients he was supposed to be transporting from one city to another had escaped. Not wanting to admit his incompetence, the driver went to a nearby bus stop and offered everyone waiting there a free ride... He then delivered the passengers to the mental hospital, telling the staff that the patients were very excitable and prone to bizarre fantasies. The deception wasn't discovered for 3 days.

5. An American teenager was in the hospital recovering from serious head wounds received from an oncoming train. When asked how he received the injuries, the lad told police that he was simply trying to see how close he could get his head to a moving train before he was hit.

6. A man walked into a Louisiana Circle-K, put a $20 bill on the counter, and asked for change. When the clerk opened the cash drawer, the man pulled a gun and asked for all the cash in the register, which the clerk promptly provided. The man took the cash from the clerk and fled, leaving the $20 bill on the counter... The total amount of cash he got from the drawer... $15. [If someone points a gun at you and gives you money, is a crime committed?]

7. Seems an Arkansas guy wanted some beer pretty badly... He decided that he'd just throw a cinder block through a liquor store window, grab some booze,

and run. So he lifted the cinder block and heaved it over his head at the window. The cinder block bounced back and hit the would-be thief on the head, knocking him unconscious. The liquor store window was made of Plexiglas. The whole event was caught on videotape...

8. As a female shopper exited a New York convenience store, a man grabbed her purse and ran. The clerk called 911 immediately, and the woman was able to give them a detailed description of the snatcher. Within minutes, the police apprehended the snatcher. They put him in the car and drove back to the store. The thief was then taken out of the car and told to stand there for a positive ID. To which he replied, "Yes, officer, that's her. That's the lady I stole the purse from."

9. A Michigan News crime column reported that a man walked into a fast food franchise in a Michigan city at 5:00

A.M., flashed a gun, and demanded cash. The clerk turned him down because he said he couldn't open the cash register without a food order. When the man ordered onion rings, the clerk said they weren't available for breakfast... The man, frustrated, walked away. [*A 5-STAR STUPIDITY AWARD WINNER]

10. When a man attempted to siphon gasoline from a motor home parked on a Portland street by sucking on a hose, he got much more than he bargained for... Police arrived at the scene to find a very sick man curled up next to a motor home near spilled sewage. A police spokesman said that the man admitted to trying to steal gasoline, but he plugged his siphon hose into the motor home's sewage tank by mistake. The owner of the vehicle declined to press charges saying that it was the best laugh he'd ever had.

In the interest of bettering mankind,

please share these with friends and family....unless of course one of these individuals by chance is a distant relative or long lost friend. In that case, be glad they are distant and hope they remain lost.

Remember.... They walk among us, and they can reproduce----*and then they VOTE !!!!*

****

In Honor of Stupid People

In case you needed further proof that the human race is doomed through stupidity, here are some *actual* label instructions on consumer goods.

On a *Sears* hairdryer -- Do not use while sleeping.

(That's the only time I have to work on my hair.)

On a bag of *Fritos* -- You could be a winner! No purchase necessary. Details inside.

(The shoplifter special?)

On a bar of *Dial* soap - "Directions: Use like regular soap."

(And that would be???....)

On some *Swanson* frozen dinners - "Serving suggestion: Defrost."

(But, it's just a suggestion.)

On *Tesco's* Tiramisu dessert (printed on bottom) -"Do not turn upside down."

(Well...duh, a bit late, huh!)

On *Marks & Spencer* Bread Pudding - "Product will be hot after heating."

(...and you thought????...)

On packaging for a *Rowenta* iron – "Do not iron clothes on body."

(But wouldn't this save me time?)

On *Boot's* Children Cough Medicine – "Do not drive a car or operate machinery after taking this medication."

(We could do a lot to reduce the rate of construction and auto accidents if we could just get those 5 & 6 year-olds with head-colds out of the cars and off those bulldozers.)

On *Nytol* Sleep Aid – "Warning: May cause drowsiness."

(...I'm taking this because???....)

On most brands of Christmas lights – "For indoor or outdoor use only."

(As opposed to what?)

On a Japanese food processor – "Not to be used for the other use."

(Now, somebody out there, help me on this. I'm a bit curious.)

On *Sainsbury's* peanuts – "Warning: contains nuts."

(Talk about a news flash- What did you expect??)

On an *American Airlines* packet of nuts – "Instructions: Open packet, eat nuts."

(Step 3: say what?)

On a child's Superman costume – "Wearing of this garment does not enable you to fly."

(I don't blame the company. I blame the parents for this one.)

On a Swedish chainsaw – "Do not attempt to stop chain with your hands or genitals."

(Oh my God…was there a lot of this happening somewhere?)

****

Other *Seriously* Bizarre Things People Did (You may not laugh at most of these) (Names of persons and cities altered)

A man in Denver, Colorado apparently got so caught up in his "Tomb Raider" computer game that he forgot he wasn't supposed to use a real gun. Sheriff's deputies confiscated Douglas Mann's shotgun after he fired it at his computer screen.

The San Bernardino, California, City Council enacted a ban on nuclear weapons, setting a $500 fine for anyone detonating one within city limits.

A company trying to continue its five-year perfect safety record showed its workers a film aimed at encouraging the use of safety goggles on the job. According to Industrial Machinery News, the film's depiction of gory industrial accidents was so graphic that twenty-five workers suffered minor injuries in their rush to leave the screening room. Thirteen others fainted, and one man required seven stitches after he cut his head falling off a chair while watching the film.

A bus carrying five passengers was hit by a car in Cincinnati, but by the time police arrived on the scene, fourteen pedestrians had boarded the bus and had begun to complain of whiplash injuries and back pain.

A doctor in Kenya successfully removed a bean lodged in a young girl's ear. According to the *Daily Nation*, when her parents told him they didn't have enough to pay his bill, the doctor "grabbed the child and forced the bean back into her ear..."

Born loser? Blame your parents. Researchers in Wales now say that your bad luck may be more than, well, bad luck. Professor Peter McMahan says you may be genetically programmed to lose. "Adverse life events," says the professor, "happen more frequently" to genetically unlucky people.

A monk in Thailand is in big trouble with local authorities and betting shops after successfully predicting the winning lottery numbers -- 11 times in a row.

A man in Pretoria, South Africa, shot his 49-year-old friend in the face, seriously wounding him, while the two practiced shooting beer cans off each other's head.

Lost your virginity? Don't worry: you can get it back. Dutch surgeons are performing the operation on adolescent girls "who are no longer virgins but wish to appear so..." fortunately, the operation is easily reversed.

Richard Schmitt of London, England somehow managed to get trapped when his own van rolled over him and pinned him to the ground. Schmitt cried out for help, but no one heard him -- no one except Sonny, a macaw parrot who lives nearby. When Sonny began to mimic the man's cries for help, two passers-by heard the parrot and freed Schmitt.

Police officers in at least four states are in cyber-trouble after exchanging explicit email messages with a 17-year-old Illinois girl. Eight deputies in North Carolina alone have been disciplined. The teen's mother says the cops "took advantage of her daughter's innocent adventures," but an attorney for one suspended officer sees it differently.

"This young woman," said Troy Spence, "has made contact with a very vulnerable element of our society -- police officers..."

Just ask your mother: researchers in Minnesota have linked poor dental hygiene to heart disease, strokes, emphysema, and premature births. Scientists warn that the bacteria in your mouth can travel through your body, putting you at risk for chronic diseases.

AT&T fired President John Walker after nine months, saying he lacked "intellectual leadership". He received a $26 million severance package. Perhaps it's not Walter who's lacking intelligence...

A 9-year-old boy in Roanoke, Virginia received a one-day suspension under his elementary school's drug policy last week - for Certs! Joey Handler allegedly told a classmate that the mints would make him "jump higher." And a student in Charleston, West Virginia was suspended for three days for giving a classmate a cough drop. School principal Forest Mann reiterated the school's "zero-tolerance" policy...not to be confused with the "zero-intelligence" policy.

Fire investigators on Maui determined the cause of a blaze that destroyed a $127,000 home the month before — a short in the homeowner's newly installed fire prevention alarm system. "This is even worse than last year," said the distraught homeowner, "when someone broke in and stole my new security system."

A man in Milan, Italy was hospitalized after swallowing 46 teaspoons, 2 cigarette lighters, and a pair of salad tongs.

More than 600 people in Italy wanted to ride in a spaceship badly enough to pay $10,000 apiece for the first tourist flight to Mars. According to the Italian police, the would-be space travelers were told to spend their "next vacation on Mars, amid the splendors of ruined temples and painted deserts. Ride a Martian camel from oasis to oasis and enjoy the incredible Martian sunsets. Explore mysterious canals and marvel at the views. Trips to the moon also available."

Authorities believe that the con men running this scam made off with over six million dollars.

A man spoke frantically into the phone: "My wife is pregnant and her contractions are only two minutes apart!"

"Is this her first child?" the doctor asked.

"No, you idiot!" the man shouted. "This is her husband!"

In Ohio, an unidentified man in his late twenties walked into a police station with a 9-inch wire protruding from his forehead, and calmly asked officers to give him an X-ray to help him find his brain, which he claimed had been stolen. Police were shocked to learn that the man had drilled a 6-inch deep hole in his skull with a top brand name power drill, and stuck the wire in to try and find the missing brain.

George Mantel, 47, of Woodside, N.Y., was camping in a remote area of the Northwest Territories when he heard "some pitter-patter sounds" outside his tent. Thinking it might be wolves, he loaded his gun and activated an emergency locator signal that is supposed to be used only for air and sea emergencies.

Authorities launched a search and rescue aircraft, whose mission cost $12,000.

Mantel, an inexperienced camper who had already burned part of his tent after a mishap with his propane heater, told rescuers he was investigating the legend of Bigfoot.

The FBI announced it is looking for Enca Sandy Kaine, 47, who had four husbands at the same time. Kay was born Eddie James Mandino and deserted from the Marine Corps nearly

30 years ago, according to FBI agent Tim Shockley, who said Mandino underwent a sex change operation two years later and changed his name.

Rabbi Yosef Cohen, the spiritual leader of Israel's Shas political party, decreed that any woman who wears a wig to a synagogue is damned. "Both she and her wig will burn in hell," Cohen said. Cohen also told followers that, contrary to popular belief, it is permissible to pick one's nose on the Sabbath.

A 25-year-old Argentine man pushed his 20-year-old wife out of an eighth-floor window after an argument, but her fall was broken when her legs became entangled in power lines below.

A police spokesperson told the state-run Telam news agency that when the husband saw the woman dangling beneath him, he apparently tried to throw himself on top of her to finish her off. He missed, however, and fell to his death. Meanwhile, the woman managed to swing over to a nearby balcony and was saved.

Young women drive almost as aggressively as men, according to an Australian study that found female drivers below age 30 are only slightly less likely than young men to tail-gate, hurl abuse, shake their fists, blast their horns and cut in front of other drivers. An aggression index, compiled from a survey by the Australian Associated Motor Insurers Ltd., shows young women scored 31.77 points on a road rage "Richter" scale, compared with men's score of 32.63.

Alan Hamm, 48, ran into a woman he knew as Linda at a gas station in Brandon, California, and invited her back to his brother's house, where they had sex. Afterward the woman reportedly made a statement implying she wanted revenge for Hamm's conviction in the 1983 murder of a friend of hers. Hamm told police the woman then cut off his penis and fled. It was found eight hours later on his front lawn, but by then it was too late to reattach the organ.

Police in Lima, Ohio, cited Kim Handle, 37, for public indecency after someone complained she was mowing her lawn topless. She put bandages and leaves on her breasts and went back to mowing the lawn.

Prosecutors dropped the indecency charge, but a judge fined Handle $40 for disorderly conduct because she turned the riding mower around in the street after drinking.

Members of the First Church of the Nazarene in Canton, Ohio, held a record burning after evangelist Jim Bowie told them that the song "A Horse is a Horse"—the theme song from the Mr. Ed show—contained satanic messages when played backwards.

Pierre Bashers, a French factory worker suffering from various obsessional fears and an inability to relate to others, decided to join a therapy group. Mr. Bashers was encouraged to sandwich himself between two mattresses, and allow other group members to walk on him to "stamp out his complexes." After several minutes of this treatment, Bashers was crushed to death.

In a related story, 9-year-old Derek Holms was run over by a 1 ton concrete roller. The boy escaped without a bruise, however, because the massive cylinder pressed him into the rain-soaked earth.

Officials from the Occupational Safety and Health Administration inspected their own offices and cited themselves on three safely violations.

French farmer Michael LePue shot himself in the foot when he opened fire on what he thought was a ghost.

Workmen in Rome, digging gravel for ballast, were instructed to dig from one central pit so as not to spoil the site with too many holes. They unearthed an ancient plaque inscribed in Latin, which turned out to be a sign intended for workman digging ballast for Roman ships. It instructed them to dig from a central pit so as not to spoil the site with too many holes.

In our 'Likely Story' department, the crew of a trawler that sank in the Sea of Japan claimed their ship went down after "being struck by a cow which fell out of the clear blue sky". According to *Flying* magazine, no one believed this absurd explanation—except the Russian military. It seems that the crew of a military cargo jet had stolen a cow they found wandering on a Siberian airfield, and loaded it aboard. While cruising at 30,000 feet, the terrified cow ran amok and jumped out of the plane.

A Florida appellate court ruled that rectal searches by police are legal. According to the Fifth District Court of Appeals, the removal of 54 grams of cocaine from a suspect's rectum by a member of the Orange County highway drug squad was "part of a legal patdown to make sure the man wasn't armed..."

In Tampa, Florida, a 70-year-old man was killed while sunbathing in a lounge chair at the beach, when a bulldozer ran over him.

The following email likely went viral.

WHEN INSULTS HAD CLASS!

These glorious insults are from an era before the English language was boiled down to 4-letter words.

·   A member of Parliament to Disraeli: "Sir, you will either die on the gallows or of some unspeakable disease."

"That depends, Sir," said Disraeli, "whether I embrace your policies or your mistress."

· "He had delusions of adequacy." - **Walter Kerr**

· "He has all the virtues I dislike and none of the vices I admire." - **Winston Churchill**

· "I have never killed a man, but I have read many obituaries with great pleasure." **Clarence Darrow**

· "He has never been known to use a word that might send a reader to the dictionary." - **William Faulkner** (about Ernest Hemingway).

· "Thank you for sending me a copy of your book; I'll waste no time reading it." - **Moses Hadas**

· "I didn't attend the funeral, but I sent a nice letter saying I approved of it." - **Mark Twain**

· "He has no enemies, but is intensely disliked by his friends.." - **Oscar Wilde**

· "I am enclosing two tickets to the first night of my new play; bring a friend, if you have one." - **George Bernard Shaw** to Winston Churchill

· "Cannot possibly attend first night, will attend second ... if there is one." - **Winston Churchill**, in response.

· "I feel so miserable without you; it's almost like having you here." - **Stephen Bishop**

· "He is a self-made man and worships his creator." - **John Bright**

· "I've just learned about his illness. Let's hope it's nothing trivial." - **Irvin S. Cobb**

· "He is not only dull himself; he is the cause of dullness in others." - **Samuel Johnson**

· "He is simply a shiver looking for a spine to run up." - **Paul Keating**

· "In order to avoid being called a flirt, she always yielded easily." - **Charles, Count Talleyrand**

· "He loves nature in spite of what it did to him." - **Forrest Tucker**

· "Why do you sit there looking like an envelope without any address on it?" - **Mark Twain**

· "His mother should have thrown him away and kept the stork." - **Mae West**

· "Some cause happiness wherever they go; others, whenever they go." - **Oscar Wilde**

· "He uses statistics as a drunken man uses lamp-posts... for support rather than illumination." - **Andrew Lang** (1844-1912)

· "He has Van Gogh's ear for music." - **Billy Wilder**

· "I've had a perfectly wonderful evening. But this wasn't it." - **Groucho Marx**

Section Six

HILARIAS REPRINTS FROM ACTUAL CHURCH BULLETINS

The sermon this morning: 'Jesus Walks on the Water.' The sermon tonight: 'Searching for Jesus.'

Ladies, don't forget the rummage sale. It's a chance to get rid of those things not worth keeping around the house. Bring your husbands.

Remember in prayer the many who are sick of our community. Smile at someone who is hard to love. Say 'Hell' to someone who doesn't care much about you.

Don't let worry kill you off - let the Church help.

Miss Charlene Mason sang 'I will not pass this way again,' giving obvious pleasure to the congregation.

For those of you who have children and don't know it, we have a nursery downstairs.

Next Thursday there will be tryouts for the choir. They need all the help they can get.

Irving Benson and Jessie Carter were married on October 24 in the church. So ends a friendship that began in their school days.

A bean supper will be held on Tuesday evening in the church hall. Music will follow...

At the evening service tonight, the sermon topic will be 'What Is Hell?' Come early and listen to our choir practice.

Eight new choir robes are currently needed due to the addition of several new members and to the deterioration of some older ones.

Scouts are saving aluminum cans, bottles and other items to be recycled. Proceeds will be used to cripple children.

Please place your donation in the envelope along with the deceased person you want remembered...

The church will host an evening of fine dining, super entertainment and gracious hostility.

Potluck supper Sunday at 5:00 PM - prayer and medication to follow.

The ladies of the Church have cast off clothing of every kind. They may be seen in the basement on Friday afternoon.

This evening at 7 PM there will be a hymn singing in the park across from the Church. Bring a blanket and come prepared to sin.

Ladies Bible Study will be held Thursday morning at 10 AM. All ladies are invited to lunch in the Fellowship Hall after the B. S. Is done.

The pastor would appreciate it if the ladies of the Congregation would lend him their electric girdles for the pancake breakfast next Sunday.

Low Self Esteem Support Group will

meet Thursday at 7 PM. Please use the back door.

The eighth-graders will be presenting Shakespeare's Hamlet in the Church basement Friday at 7 PM. The congregation is invited to attend this tragedy.

Weight Watchers will meet at 7 PM at the First Presbyterian Church. Please use large double door at the side entrance.

The Associate Minister unveiled the church's new campaign slogan last Sunday: 'I Upped My Pledge - Up Yours.

BONUS: CATHOLIC SHAMPOO

TWO NUNS WERE SHOPPING AT A
7-11 STORE. AS THEY PASSED BY
THE BEER COOLER,
ONE NUN SAID TO THE OTHER,
"WOULDN'T A NICE COOL BEER OR
TWO TASTE
WONDERFUL ON A HOT SUMMER
EVENING?"

THE SECOND NUN
ANSWERED, "INDEED IT WOULD,
SISTER, BUT I WOULD NOT FEEL
COMFORTABLE BUYING BEER,
SINCE I AM CERTAIN IT WOULD
CAUSE A SCENE AT THE CHECKOUT
STAND."

"I CAN HANDLE THAT WITHOUT
A PROBLEM" THE OTHER NUN
REPLIED, AND SHE PICKED UP A
SIX-PACK AND HEADED FOR THE
CHECK-OUT.

THE CASHIER HAD A SURPRISED LOOK ON HIS FACE WHEN THE TWO NUNS ARRIVED WITH A SIX-PACK OF BEER. "WE USE BEER FOR WASHING OUR HAIR" THE NUN SAID, "BACK AT OUR NUNNERY, WE CALL IT CATHOLIC SHAMPOO.

WITHOUT BLINKING AN EYE, THE CASHIER REACHED UNDER THE COUNTER. PULLED OUT A PACKAGE OF PRETZEL STICKS, AND PLACED THEM IN THE BAG WITH THE BEER.

HE THEN LOOKED THE NUN STRAIGHT IN THE EYE, SMILED, AND SAID: "THE CURLERS ARE ON THE HOUSE."

Section Seven

SHARING

A lotta pun

I changed my iPod's name to Titanic. Now it's syncing.

When chemists die, they barium.

Jokes about German sausage are the wurst kind.

I know a guy who's addicted to brake fluid. He says he can stop any time.

How does Moses make his tea? Hebrews it.

I stayed up all night to see where the sun went. Then it dawned on me.

This girl said she recognized me from the vegetarian club, but I'd never met herbivore.

I'm reading a book about anti-gravity. I just can't put it down.

I did a theatrical performance about puns. It was a play on words.

They told me I had type-A blood, but it was a type-O.

PMS jokes aren't funny. Period.

We are going on a class trip to the Coca-Cola factory. I hope there's no pop quiz.

I didn't like my beard at first. Then it grew on me.

Did you hear about the cross-eyed teacher who lost her job because she couldn't control her pupils?

When you get a bladder infection, urine trouble.

Broken pencils are really pointless.

I tried to catch some fog, but I mist.

What do you call a dinosaur with an extensive vocabulary? The saurus.

England has no kidney bank, but it does have a Liverpool.

I used to be a banker, but then I lost interest.

I dropped out of Communism class because of lousy Marx.

All the toilets in New York's police stations have been stolen. The police have nothing to go on.

I got a job at a bakery because I kneaded dough.

Haunted French pancakes give me the crepes.

A cartoonist was found dead in his home. Details are sketchy.

Venison for dinner again? Oh deer!

The earthquake in Washington was obviously the government's fault.

Be kind to your dentist. He has fillings, too.

Velcro. What a rip off!

Limericks, Jokes and Other Such Rubbish

Section
Eight

In the Military that's nuts;

here it's just laughable

Just had to include these

While I sat in the reception area of my doctor's office, a woman rolled an elderly man in a wheelchair into the room. As she went to the receptionist's desk, the man sat there, alone and silent. Just as I was thinking I should make small talk with him, a little boy slipped off his mother's lap and walked over to the wheelchair. Placing his hand on the man's, he said, "I know how you feel. My Mom makes me ride in the stroller too."

****

As I was nursing my baby, my cousin's six-year-old daughter, Krissy, came into the room. Never having seen anyone breast feed before, she was intrigued and full of all kinds of questions about what I was doing. After mulling over my answers, she remarked, "My mom has some of those, but I don't think she knows how to use them."

****

Out bicycling one day with my eight-year-old granddaughter, Carolyn, I got a little wistful. "In ten years," I said, "you'll want to be with your friends and you won't go walking, biking, and swimming with me like you do now.

Carolyn shrugged. "In ten years you'll be too old to do all those things anyway."

****

Working as a pediatric nurse, I had the difficult assignment of giving immunization shots to children. One day, I entered the examining room to give four-year-old Lizzie her injection.

"No, no, no!" she screamed.

"Lizzie," scolded her mother, "that's not polite behavior."

With that, the girl yelled even louder, "No, thank you! No, thank you!

****

On the way back from a Cub Scout meeting, my grandson innocently said to my son, "Dad, I know babies come from mommies" tummies, but how do they get there in the first place?"

After my son hemmed and hawed awhile, my grandson finally spoke up in disgust, "You don't have to make up something, Dad. It's okay if you don't know the answer."

****

Just before I was deployed to Iraq, I sat my eight-year-old son down and broke the news to him. "I'm going to be away for a long time," I told him. "I'm going to Iraq."

"Why?" he asked. "Don't you know there's a war going on over there?"

****

Paul Newman founded the Hole in the Wall Gang Camp for children stricken with cancer, AIDS, and blood diseases.

One afternoon, he and is wife, Joanne Woodward, stopped by to have lunch with the kids. A counselor at a nearby table, suspecting the young patients wouldn't know Newman was a famous movie star, explained, "That's the man who made this camp possible. Maybe you've seen his picture on his salad dressing bottle?"

Blank stares.

"Well, you've probably seen his face on his lemonade carton."

An eight-year-old girl perked up. "How long was he missing?"

****

God's Problem Now!

His wife's graveside service was just barely finished, when there was a massive clap of thunder, followed by a tremendous bolt of lightning, accompanied by even more thunder rumbling in the distance. The little, old man looked at the pastor and calmly said, "Well, she's there."

****

After dying in a car crash, three friends go to Heaven for orientation. They are all asked the same question: "When you are in your casket, and friends and family are mourning over you, what would you like to hear them say about you?"

The first guy immediately responds, "I would like to hear them say that I was one of the great doctors of my time, and a great family man."

The second guy says, "I would like to hear that I was a wonderful husband and school teacher who made a huge difference in our children of tomorrow."

The last guy thinks a minute and replies, "I'd like to hear them say......LOOK, HE'S MOVING!!!!!"

****

You Don't Need to Be a Weatherman...
It was two o'clock in the morning and a husband and wife were asleep, when suddenly the phone rang. The husband picked up the phone and said, "Hello? ... How the heck do I know? What am I, the weather man?" and promptly slammed the phone down. His wife rolls over and asks, "Who was that?" The husband replies, I don't know. Some guy who wanted to know if the coast was clear."

****

An army officer had just returned to the U.S. from Afghanistan, where he had lost an ear when a mine exploded. Anxious to regroup, he surveyed his troops for a candidate to name as second in command. After carefully selecting three sharp young soldiers, he called each one in separately to test them for the job.

"Do you notice anything different about me since I returned?" he asked the first.

"Certainly, sir," he said bluntly, "You're missing one ear."
"That will be all, private," said the officer, calling in the next.

"Do you notice anything different about me, soldier?" he again queried.

"Yes, sir, I was wondering if you can hear out of the ear that is missing."

"Dismissed!" the officer snapped, summoning the final man.

After being asked the same question, the young man said softly, "You're not wearing eyeglasses."

"The officer began to smile. "You are right," he said with a nod.

"Well," continued the soldier, "It would be a bit hard to wear glasses when you're missing one of your freaking ears!"

****

A young boy had noticed for some time that he didn't favor his sister and what was worse, the sister favored both parents and he favored neither. Finally he got up the nerve to ask his mother if he had been adopted.

The mother suddenly burst out crying. "Yes, son," she managed between sobs, "but it didn't work out and they brought you back!"

****

A Baptist preacher was doing neighborhood visitation to invite folks out to Sunday morning services. One man informed him that he was a producer of fine peach brandy. He told the pastor that he would attend his church the following Sunday if he would drink a glass of his brandy and admit to his congregation that Sunday morning that he had done so. The minister agreed and gurgled down the brandy.

Sunday morning, as the man smugly watched from a seat near the front of the sanctuary, the pastor spoke up, "I see Mr. Jones in here with us this morning! I wish to thank him publically for his kind hospitality this week and particularly for the peaches he gave me and the spirit in which they were given."

****

Judge's tie

At a thrift shop the wife of a federal district court judge bought a green tie which perfectly matched one of her husband's sports jackets. Shortly afterward they were vacationing in a resort to get their minds off of a

particularly   troubling   cocaine
conspiracy case. While attending a party
at which the tie was worn, the judge
noticed a small round disc sewn into the
design of the tie. Afraid that it might be
a bug placed there by the conspiracy
defendants, he showed it to an F.B.I.
agent who sent it to Washington
headquarters to be examined.

"It's impossible to determine where this
disc came from," the examiner told the
agent, "but it plays Jingle Bells when
you press it."

****

Buy your own presents

A grandmother had gotten tired of the
Christmas shopping crowds, plus the
fact that she never knew what her ever-
changing grandchildren would like. So,
she decided one Christmas just send
them all a check and let them make the
proper choice of gifts.

She wrote the checks and made out cards, each with the following note, which she mailed to the grandkids:

"Buy your own gifts this year."

After Christmas she opened her desk drawer, and there, to her chagrin, were all of the checks to the grand kids — oops!

Section Nine

**Twenty-five great truths from
smart people
(Some may not seem so
funny)**

1. In my many years I have come to a conclusion that one useless man is a shame, two is a law firm and three or more is a congress. -- **John Adams**

2. If you don't read the newspaper you are uninformed, if you do read the newspaper you are misinformed. -- **Mark Twain**

3. Suppose you were an idiot. And suppose you were a member of Congress. But then I repeat myself. -- **Mark Twain**

4. I contend that for a nation to try to tax itself into prosperity is like a man standing in a bucket and trying to lift himself up by the handle. -- **Winston Churchill**

5. A government which robs Peter to pay Paul can always depend on the support of Paul. -- **George Bernard Shaw**

6. A liberal is someone who feels a great debt to his fellow man, which debt he proposes to pay off with your money. -- **G. Gordon Liddy**

7. Democracy must be something more than two wolves and a sheep voting on what to have for dinner. -- **James Bovard**, Civil Libertarian (1994)

8. Foreign aid might be defined as a transfer of money from poor people in rich countries to rich people in poor countries. -- **Douglas Casey**, Classmate of Bill Clinton at George- town University

9. Giving money and power to government is like giving whiskey and car keys to teenage boys. -- **P.J. O'Rourke**, Civil Libertarian

10. Government is the great fiction, through which everybody endeavors to live at the expense of everybody else. --

Frederic Bastiat, French economist (1801-1850)

11. Government's view of the economy could be summed up in a few short phrases: If it moves, tax it. If it keeps moving, regulate it. And if it stops moving, subsidize it. -- **Ronald Reagan** (1986)

12. I don't make jokes. I just watch the government and report the facts. -- **Will Rogers**

13. If you think health care is expensive now, wait until you see what it costs when it's free! -- **P.J. O'Rourke**

14. In general, the art of government consists of taking as much money as possible from one party of the citizens to give to the other. -- **Voltaire** (1764)

15. Just because you do not take an interest in politics doesn't mean politics

won't take an interest in you! --
Pericles (430 B.C.)

16. No man's life, liberty, or property is
safe while the legislature is in session. --
Mark Twain (1866)

17. Talk is cheap...except when Congress
does it. -- **Anonymous**

18. The government is like a baby's
alimentary canal, with a happy appetite
at one end and no responsibility at the
other. -- **Ronald Reagan**

19. The inherent vice of capitalism is the
unequal sharing of the blessings. The
inherent blessing of socialism is the
equal sharing of misery. -- **Winston
Churchill**

20. The only difference between a tax
man and a taxidermist is that the
taxidermist leaves the skin. --**Mark
Twain**

21. The ultimate result of shielding men from the effects of folly is to fill the world with fools. -- **Herbert Spencer** , English Philosopher (1820-1903)

22. There is no distinctly Native American criminal class...save Congress. -- **Mark Twain**

23. What this country needs are more unemployed politicians. -- **Edward Langley** , Artist (1928-1995)

24. A government big enough to give you everything you want, is strong enough to take everything you have. -- **Thomas Jefferson**

25. We hang the petty thieves and appoint the great ones to public office. -- **Aesop**

Section Ten

WHY MEN ARE NEVER DEPRESSED
and other gender differences

More passed along thoughts

Men Are Just Happier People --

What do you expect from such simple
creatures?
Your last name stays put.
The garage is all yours.
Wedding plans take care of themselves.
Chocolate is just another snack...
You can never be pregnant.
You can wear a white T-shirt to a water
park.
You can wear NO shirt to a water park.
Car mechanics tell you the truth.
The world is your urinal.
You don't have to stop and think of
which way to turn a nut on a bolt.
Same work, more pay.
Wrinkles add character.
Wedding dress $5000. Tux rental-$100.
People never stare at your chest when
you're talking to them.
New shoes don't cut, blister, or mangle
your feet.
One mood all the time.
Phone conversations are over in 30
seconds flat.

A five-day vacation requires only one suitcase.

You can open all your own jars.

You get extra credit for the slightest act of thoughtfulness.

If someone forgets to invite you, he or she can still be your friend.

Your underwear is $8.95 for a three-pack.

Three pairs of shoes are more than enough...

You are unable to see wrinkles in your clothes...

Everything on your face stays its original color.

The same hairstyle lasts for years, even decades.

You only have to shave your face and neck.

You can play with toys all your life.

One wallet and one pair of shoes -- one color for all seasons.

You can wear shorts no matter how your legs look.

Men Are Just Happier People

NICKNAMES

If Laura, Kate and Sarah go out for lunch, they will call each other Laura, Kate and Sarah.

If Mike, Dave and John go out, they will affectionately refer to each other as Fat Boy, Bubba and Wildman.

EATING OUT

When the bill arrives, Mike, Dave and John will each throw in $20, even though it's only for $32.50.

None of them will have anything smaller and none will actually admit they want change back.

When the girls get their bill, out come the pocket calculators.

MONEY

A man will pay $2 for a $1 item he needs.

A woman will pay $1 for a $2 item that she doesn't need but it's on sale.

BATHROOMS

A man has six items in his bathroom: toothbrush and toothpaste,

shaving cream, razor, a bar of soap, and a towel.
The average number of items in the typical woman's bathroom is 337.
A man would not be able to identify more than 20 of these items.

ARGUMENTS

A woman has the last word in any argument.

Anything a man says after that is the beginning of a new argument.

FUTURE

A woman worries about the future until she gets a husband.

A man never worries about the future until he gets a wife.

MARRIAGE

A woman marries a man expecting he will change, but he doesn't.

A man marries a woman expecting that she won't change, but she does.

DRESSING UP

A woman will dress up to go shopping, water the plants, empty the trash, answer the phone, read a book, and get the mail.

A man will dress up for weddings and funerals.

NATURAL

Men wake up as good-looking as they went to bed.

Women somehow deteriorate during the night.

OFFSPRING

Ah, children. A woman knows all about her children.

She knows about dentist appointments and romances, best friends, favorite foods, secret fears and hopes and dreams.

A man is vaguely aware of some short people living in the house.

AND FINALLY, REMEMBER: If a man says he'll fix something, he will. There's no need to remind him every six months about it.

Limericks, Jokes and Other Such Rubbish

Section Eleven

More 'plumb funny'
passed along jokes

Martin impresses his Sunday School teacher

Martin arrived at Sunday School late. Miss Brown, his teacher, knew that Martin was usually punctual, so she asked him if anything was wrong.

"No," Martin replied, "I had been going fishing but my dad told me I needed to go to church."

Miss Brown was very impressed. "Did your dad explain to you why it was more important to go to church than to go fishing?"

"Yeah, he did," Martin grinned. "Dad said he didn't have enough bait for both of us."

****

Inner Peace

I think I've found inner peace. My therapist told me the way to achieve inner peace was to finish things I had started.

Today I finished two bags of potato chips, a dozen chocolate chip cookies. Four Reese's Cups, a lemon pie, a fifth of Jack Daniels and a box of chocolate candy.

I feel better already.

****

The Senility Prayer

God, grant me the senility to forget the people I never liked anyway, the good fortune to run into the ones I do, and the eyesight to know the difference.

Lucky saucer

In the front of a butcher's shop a collector of antiques noticed a scraggly little kitten lapping milk from a saucer. Not just any saucer — this one, he realized, was a rare and valuable collector's item.

Strolling nonchalantly into the store, he offered the butcher five dollars for the tiny, shabby feline.

"He's not for sale," said the butcher with a frown.

"Look," the collector protested, "that cat is dirty and mangy-looking, but I'm an eccentric. I like cats that way. I'll give you twenty dollars."

"It's a deal," agreed the shop owner, cramming the bill in his pocket immediately.

"For that amount of money I'm sure you won't mind throwing in the saucer," said the collector. "The kitten seems so happy drinking from it."

"No can do!" said the butcher in a firm tone. "That's my lucky saucer. So far this week I've sold eighteen cats."

****

Ethnic joke:

An Englishman, a Scotsman, an Irishman, a Welshman, a Latvian, a Turk, a German, an Indian, several Americans (including a Hawaiian and an Alaskan), an Argentinean, a Dane, an Australian, a Slovak, an Egyptian, a Japanese, a Moroccan, a Frenchman, a New Zealander, a Spaniard, a Russian, a Guatemalan, a Colombian, a Pakistani, a
Malaysian, a Croatian, a Uzbek, a Cypriot, a Pole, a Lithuanian, a Chinese, a Sri Lankan, a Lebanese, a Cayman Islander, a Ugandan, a

Vietnamese, a Korean, a Uruguayan, a Czech, an Icelander, a Mexican, a Finn, a Honduran, a Panamanian, an Andorran, an Israeli, a Venezuelan, an Iranian, a Fijian, a Peruvian, an Estonian, a Syrian, a Brazilian, a Portuguese, a Liechtensteiner, a Mongolian, a Hungarian, a Canadian, a Moldovan, a Haitian, a Norfolk Islander, a Macedonian, a Bolivian, a Cook Islander, a Tajikistani, a Samoan, an Armenian, an Aruban, an Albanian, a Greenlander, a Micronesian, a Virgin Islander, a Georgian, a Bahaman, a Belarusian, a Cuban, a Tongan, a Cambodian, a Canadian, a Qatari, an Azerbaijani, a Romanian, a Chilean, a Jamaican, a Filipino, a Ukrainian, a Dutchman, a Ecuadorian, a Costa Rican, a Swede, a Bulgarian, a Serb, a Swiss, a Greek, a Belgian, a Singaporean, an Italian, a Norwegian and 2 Africans

...Walk into a fine restaurant.

"I'm sorry," says the maître d', after

scrutinizing the group, "You can't come in here without a Thai."

Limericks, Jokes and Other Such Rubbish

Section Twelve

Did I mention that she was blonde?

Getting a blonde to laugh

How do you make a blonde laugh on Monday?

Tell her a joke on Friday!

****

Will he or won't he"

A blonde and a redhead went to the bar after work for a drink, and sat down on stools watching the 6:00 o'clock news. A man was shown threatening to jump from the Brooklyn Bridge, and the blonde bet the redhead $50 that he wouldn't jump.

Sure enough, he jumped, so the blonde gave the redhead $50. The redhead said, "I can't take this, you're my friend."

But the blonde insisted saying, "No. A bet's a bet."

Then the redhead said, "Listen, I have to tell you that I saw this on the 5:00 o'clock news, so I can't take your money."

The blonde answered back, "Well, so did I, but I didn't think he would jump again!"

****

Blonde Atlanta Bound

On a plane bound for Atlanta the flight attendant approached a blonde sitting in the first class section and requested that she move to coach since she did not have a first class ticket.

The blonde replied, "I'm blonde, I'm beautiful, I'm going to Atlanta, and I'm not moving."

Not wanting to argue with a customer, the flight attendant asked the co-pilot to speak with her. He went to talk with the woman asking her to please move out of the first class section.

Again, the blonde replied, "I'm blonde, I'm beautiful, I'm going to Atlanta, and I'm not moving."

The co-pilot returned to the cockpit and asked the captain what he should do.

The captain said, "I'm married to a blonde, and I know how to handle this." He went to the first class section and whispered in the blonde's ear. She immediately jumped up and ran to the coach section mumbling to herself, "Why didn't anyone just say so."

Surprised, the flight attendant and the co-pilot asked what he said to her that finally convinced her to move from her seat.

The pilot replied, "I told her the first class section wasn't going to Atlanta."

****

Longest password

During a company audit of passwords, the Communications Exec discovered that a young lady was using the following password: "MickeyMinniePlutoLouisDeweyGoofy Sacra- mento"

"Why on earth are you using such a long password?" the Exec asked.

"Hello! It has to be at least 8 characters and include at least one capital," she said, batting her long lashes.

Yep, she was blonde.

****

I just asked a simple question!

A blonde asked someone what time it was, and they told her it was 4:30. The blonde got a puzzled look.

"You know, it's the weirdest thing, I've been asking that question all day, and each time I get a different answer."

****

Cheerio!

Question: What did the blonde say when she opened the box of Cherios?

Answer: "Oh, look! Little donut seeds!"

****

Blondes in a Parking Lot

Two blondes were in a parking lot trying to unlock the door of their Mercedes with a coat hanger. They tried and tried to get the door open, but they couldn't.

The girl with the coat hanger stopped for a moment to catch her breath, and her friend said anxiously, "Hurry up! It's starting to rain and the top is down."

****

That smarts!

Question: What do you call a blonde with a 50 I.Q.?

Answer: Gifted.

****

The Blonde and the Handgun

A young blonde woman is distraught because she fears her husband is having an affair, so she goes to a gun shop and buys a handgun. The next day she comes home to find her husband in bed with a beautiful redhead. She grabs the gun and holds it to her own head. The husband jumps out of bed, begging and pleading with her not to shoot herself.

Hysterically the blonde responds to the husband, "Shut up... you're next!"

****

The blonde and the grenade

Question: What do you do when a blonde throws a hand grenade at you?

Answer: Pull the pin and throw it back.

****

Too much pizza

The waitress asked a blonde if she would like her pizza cut into six pieces or twelve.

"Six please" she said, "I could never eat twelve!"

****

Believe it or not

Question: What do an intelligent blonde and a UFO have in common?

Answer: No matter how often you hear about them, you never see one.

****

Two coats

A man went into the office kitchen one morning and found a new blonde girl painting the walls wearing a new fur coat and a nice denim jacket.

Thinking this was a little odd he asked her why she was wearing them instead of old clothes or overalls.

She showed him the instructions on the paint can:

For best results, put on two coats.

****

Let's get hitched

Question: How do you get a dumb blonde to marry you?

Answer: Tell her she's pregnant.

****

Just following instructions

A man had a blind date with a blonde. When he picked her up, he thought it odd that she had headphones on and wouldn't take them off when he asked her to. Finally he reached over and removed them. Soon, her head fell to her shoulders, and he could see she was not breathing. Quickly he grabbed the headphones and listened to the incessant recording:
"Breathe in, breathe out, breathe in, breathe out..."

****

Are you sure?

Question: What did the dumb blonde say to the doctor when she found out she was pregnant?

Answer: "Are you sure it's mine?"

****

Quick! Call 911!

Shortly after the 911 emergency number became available, an elderly and quite ill blonde appeared in a New York hospital emergency room, having driven herself to the hospital and barely managing to stagger in from the parking lot.

The horrified nurse said, "Why didn't you call the 911 number and get an ambulance?"

The lady replied, "My phone doesn't have an eleven!"

****

Blonde Prison Break

A blonde, brunette, and a redhead escaped from prison. They were running along when they came upon a dock. On the dock were three gunnysacks. They could hear the cops approaching, so the brunette suggested that they get in the sacks. So they got in the sacks right before the cops arrived.

A cop kicked the sack with the redhead in it, and she said, "Ruff ruff ruff!"

He said, "Oh, it's only a dog."

He kicked the one with the brunette in it, and she said "Meow meow meow."

He said, "Oh, it's only a cat."
Then, he kicked the one with the blonde in it, and she said, "POTATOES POTATOES POTATOES!"

****

A penny for your thoughts

Question: What do you get when you offer a blonde a penny for her thoughts?

Answer: Change.

****

Showing her true colors

A dumb blonde was really tired of being made fun of, so she decided to have her hair dyed so everyone would think she was a brunette.

Once she had brown hair, she decided to take a drive through the country.

After she had been driving for a while, she saw a farmer and a flock of sheep and thought,

Oh! Those sheep are so adorable!
She got out and walked over the farmer and said, "If I can guess how

many sheep you have, can I take one home?"

The farmer, being a bit of a gambler himself, said she could have a try.

The blonde looked around the flock and then guessed, "157."

The farmer was amazed — she was right! So the blonde, (who looked like a brunette), picked one out and put it into her car.
Before she left, the farmer walked up to her and asked, "If I can guess the real color of your hair, can I have my dog back?"

****

Playing tag

Question: How many blondes does it take to play tag?

Answer: One.

****

What happened?

Did you hear about the blondes who froze to death at the drive-in? They went to see "Closed for the Winter."

****

Falling off a building

Question: If a blonde and a brunette fell off a building, who would hit the ground first?

Answer: The brunette - the blonde would have to stop for directions!

****

Right guard

A blonde had just packed her husband's toiletries and clothes for a trip. On the way out the driveway she said, "Honey, we need to stop at a store and get you some left guard."

"What the heck are you talking about?" he asked.

"Well," she answered, when I was packing your deodorant I noticed all you had was right guard. You need something for the other side."

****

Natural born blonde

In a high school civics class the qualifications for running for President of the U.S. were being discussed. Quite simply, the candidate must be a natural born citizen and at least thirty-five years of age.

A blonde student became irate about how unfair this was stating that many qualified persons would be eliminated with these rules.

Finally she snapped, "What makes a natural born citizen more qualified than one born by C-Section?"